One Calling Many Vocations

M. Ann Bruening
Eph 6:10-13

One Calling Many Vocations

I'll Be a Friend to Jesus

Gilbert N. Hulme
Mary Ann Bruening

PROVIDENCE HOUSE PUBLISHERS
Franklin, Tennessee

Scripture taken from the KING JAMES VERSION

Printed in the United States of America

00 99 98 97 96 5 4 3 2 1

Library of Congress Catalog Card Number: 96–70899

ISBN: 1–57736–027–3

Cover design by Benjamin T. Bruening

PROVIDENCE HOUSE PUBLISHERS
238 Seaboard Lane • Franklin, Tennessee 37067
800-321-5692

To Jesus Christ
the Friend above all friends

"Greater love hath no man than this,
that a man lay down his life for his friends.
Ye are my friends, if ye do
whatsoever I command you."

John 15:13–14

CONTENTS

ACKNOWLEDGMENTS

CREDIT FOR THIS BOOK MUST RIGHTFULLY BE given to my mother, Lillis Hulme. She laboriously copied the original notes for my dad when he was too weak to accomplish the task himself. She then encouraged me with her advice and with endless reading and rereading to proof the many drafts. Most of all, I thank her for her love and faithfulness, first to my dad, and then to her children. She is truly an example of a gracious, Christian lady.

I owe a debt of thanks to my schoolteacher friends who have encouraged me to complete this book and who have also helped in refining the text. I especially express thanks to Evelyn Sangster for her invaluable input; to my college professor, Jenny Cramer; to my very capable paraprofessional, Phyllis Masters; and to my mentor and friend, Mary Jane Lybyer. I am grateful for the encouragement of a very special friend, Gail Hall, who helped me see the ministry God intended in the conception of this writing.

And most of all, I owe a debt of thanks to the wonderful partner and friend whom God gave me in my husband, Harold Bruening. He has always seen the best in me and has encouraged me to be all that God intended. Without his support and encouragement throughout the years, this book could not have been written.

To each of these, I extend my humble thanks for whatever part you have had in my life.

—Mary Ann Bruening

INTRODUCTION

THIS BOOK BEGAN AS THE STORY OF ONE MAN'S journey to a pastoral calling; but in the account of his journey, the story of one of his children also emerges. And so in the reading, it may become the story of many who have met Jesus while young and who have committed themselves to serve him in a special way.

The story is written as an encouragement for those who have dared to aspire to dreams that seem unattainable. As it was with Abraham, Moses, and even Jesus, the circumstances of life may delay one's commitment. It may take years of preparation to get to the ultimate time and place where God's perfect plan will come into clear focus. Forty years in various vocations were needed to prepare this preacher for the next forty years of action.

The preacher encourages those who may find themselves in this book with these words: "So, my fellow traveler, do not be discouraged. Sometimes it takes one-half of a lifetime in close fellowship with Christ to reach the completion of full surrender to the calling of our Good Shepherd, Jesus. It is not necessary to see the total picture in the beginning. Just put your trust in the Master and commit to him. Be a friend to Jesus and go wherever he leads."

—Gilbert N. Hulme

He has shewed thee, O man, what is good; and what doth the Lord require of thee, but to do justly, and to love mercy, and to walk humbly with thy God?

—Micah 6:8

Chapter

One

IT WAS OCTOBER 5, 1908, AUTUMN IN THE ROLLING hills of north Georgia. Surrounding the little cabin were trees in brilliant hues of red and orange and gold. The months had seemed endless as the family had waited and prepared for the blessed event that was now imminent.

These were hard times leading into what would be known as the Great Depression. Everyone had his own place in this farm home. All pitched in to do the job that had to be done. Everyone, from the black servant who cared for the small children and helped with household chores to the hands who helped work the cotton fields, worked hard. For cotton was still "king" in this poor farming community. Growing cotton made it possible for families to keep food on the table and to maintain their strong pride that had been handed down for generations.

Finally the cry came! What a time for rejoicing this was! A beautiful baby boy had been born with black hair that spoke of his Cherokee ancestry and sky blue eyes that already sparkled with intelligence. This son would certainly be able to help with the hard work found on the farm. He could assume his dad's role as was the tradition of the time. Or perhaps he would be the preacher man for whom his mother aspired. Maybe he would teach others. He would surely bring honor to the family name.

Little baby, what do you see?
When you grow up, what will you be?
Born in a cabin, surroundings small,
You will stand with kings when you
follow his call.

When Jesus calls, what will you do?
Will you love him for life,
with service true?
Will you be His friend, or will you be His foe
To the precious One who loves you so?

Many were the beautiful and lofty thoughts flooding the little cabin the day this baby was ushered into a world of love and beauty to accept his destiny.

CHAPTER

Two

THE YEARS PASSED BY SO VERY QUICKLY. THE boy learned much. The kindly woman who attended him delighted in telling Bible stories from the Good Book. He was quick to learn and ever begged for more. He loved to hear of Moses who took a whole nation out of slavery and crossed a big sea. He heard of a boy named Daniel who survived in a den of lions because he loved God. There was David who killed a big giant and Jonah who got swallowed by a whale. And with every story, there was a thought to store away, to ponder, until the time that it would be needed to live life as God intended.

The stories that this boy loved most were those that were told about a man named Jesus. He did so many wonderful things. He made sick people get well, and he made blind people see. He made lots of food out of just one little boy's lunch, and he always had time for little children.

Sunday was a favorite day because no one labored on that day. The whole family went to the little country church. They sang wonderful songs about Jesus.

But one Sunday was different in a world of sameness. The boy was still very young, but he was always listening and thinking. The ideas that would guide his life were nearly formed as he very methodically put each new piece of evidence in its own place. This particular Sunday, though, the words from one of the songs in church stopped him short. They just didn't make sense:

They tried my Lord and Master,
With no one to defend;
Within the halls of Pilate
He stood without a friend.

The questions flooded inward. How could anyone not be a friend to Jesus? This man was the hero of all heroes. He even died for us—for each one of us.

Even after the family had gone home, the boy remained outside to ponder this great perplexity. As he stood there in his yard beside the 1914 family car, this boy, only six years old, quietly made his decision. Looking skyward, he answered the quiet prompting of the Holy Spirit with this commitment: "I'll be a friend to Jesus. I'll follow his calling whatever it may be."

The words of the song were to echo in his heart throughout the rest of his life:

The world may turn against Him,
I'll love Him to the end,
And while on earth I'm living,
My Lord shall have a friend.

I'll do what He may bid me;
I'll go where He may send;
I'll try each flying moment
To prove that I'm His friend.

I'll be a friend to Jesus,
My life for Him I'll spend;
I'll be a friend to Jesus,
Until my years shall end.*

*Johnson Oatman and J. W. Dennis, *Favorite Songs and Hymns*, Stamps-Baxter Music Company, 1939 ("I'll Be a Friend to Jesus," p. 156).

Chapter

Three

THE GEORGIA FARM BOY CONTINUED TO GROW. He soon started going to grammar school and showed much ability as he continued to question and to acquire knowledge.

He spent much time roaming the beautiful and beloved hills surrounding his home. He loved the sound of rushing water as streams and rivers flowed abundantly nearby. Fishing was a favorite pastime because it made him feel close to his friend Jesus. He liked to think what it would have been like to have lived back in Bible times.

Music was an integral part of the southern lifestyle. People sang on any occasion. Real instruments were not always available, but the mountain people had long since learned to improvise.

It was nothing out of the ordinary for him to hear someone play an old handsaw with a violin bow. But for this boy, the fascination was more than a novelty as he determined to try it for himself. It did not take long for him to begin to draw out the unusual and beautiful tones. His favorite hymns took on new meaning as he expressed those innermost thoughts through the message of the saw.

A barefoot boy with eyes of blue
Sat 'neath the Georgia sky,
And music played from all the earth
To be used in the by-and-by.

So many tunes stored there to know
Just waiting for time to show;
To surface in art form old as those hills,
The music he found in the rocks and rills.

When he tired of the discipline of practicing his music, there were always chores around the farm. He enjoyed fixing and creating with the practical side of his instrument.

In this way, the saw became a special link that added spiritual meaning to life with his friend Jesus. As he worked, he often thought about Jesus who was himself a carpenter in his father's shop.

At age twelve, the young man decided it was time to tell others about his unique friendship. Following the example of Abraham, the patriarch of Israel who expressed faith in God, the young man made public his faith in Jesus.

Abraham believed God,
and it was imputed unto him for righteousness:
and he was called the Friend of God.

—James 2:23

The Georgia teenager herewith made a public commitment to spend his life as a minister of the gospel.

CHAPTER

FOUR

NOT LONG AFTER HIS PUBLIC DECISION, THE boy graduated from the country grammar school. It had been a difficult task to complete those first eight years of education. The first obligation was always to the farm. Crops must be put in, tended, and harvested. There was livestock to feed. The school was some five miles away. It took a long time to walk that distance, for there was not always transportation. Even the mules owned by the family could not be spared to spend the day at school. Even so, the boy studied every spare moment. It was not unusual to see him at the end of a row of cotton with a book in hand as he and the mule grabbed a few minutes of rest.

After graduation, the days on the farm grew into months and months into years. Dreams of higher education that would prepare for ministry were never far away. Although the family supported the young man's goals, high school required tuition, and there was never enough money. Public high school and government assistance were far in the future.

The young man was willing, but his dreams seemed to be forever out of his grasp. Often, he wondered whether his friend Jesus would make his goals reality. At every opportunity, he would sing in the country church or speak for his Lord.

As the man endured many days of discouragement, he realized that the circumstances of life often dictate our direction. Whether or not he could ever attain the higher education he so dearly sought, he knew that nothing could prevent his continued friendship with Jesus. That friendship carried him onward.

CHAPTER

FIVE

THE PRAYERS OF THE YOUNG MAN TO BE USED in ministry were being answered as God so often answers prayers, in the form of another person, a wealthy young woman who was following her own call to ministry. The exciting news finally came.

There was a teacher who lived in Rome, Georgia, who had started a school for mountain children. She had a dream that school should be available for anyone. She accepted deserving students and allowed them to work in lieu of payment. Her name was Martha Berry.

The young man could think of nothing else. His father said, "Son, I have eighty-six dollars which will pay your travel expenses to Rome to the Berry School. You can go if you are accepted."

The boy was accepted. As he studied, he helped plant crops and work the fields at the school. He enjoyed the opportunities to sing in the college quartet. As he often walked past the big house on the hill where his benefactor, Miss Berry, lived, he marveled at the wonderful grace of God that allowed such opportunity to a poor country farm boy.

One day as he was plowing in the Berry School fields, a terrible accident took place. The horse broke away, knocked the young man to the ground, and pulled the harrow over his helpless body. He was quickly loaded in the back of a wagon and taken to the hospital. The damage was massive; a broken jaw and mangled leg were pieced together. The doctor sadly shook his head as he pronounced that this young man would never be able to talk or walk again.

When medical science could do no more, the prayers of God's people took over. "Please, God," the young man prayed, "let me talk and sing and walk again that I may bring glory to your Name."

No doctor could explain the miracle that began to happen as the injuries slowly healed and the young man was able to resume his duties at school with renewed vigor. What seemed to be tragedy in the unfortunate accident was turned to victory as God continued to train his servant as he worked his way through Berry High School and continued there for two additional years of Bible training.

CHAPTER

SIX

A FIRST VOCATION IS SELDOM AN EASY CHOICE. The man was faced with several roads toward useful and meaningful kinds of work. One such opportunity was to serve as an apprentice in a funeral home. As the young man conversed with his friend Jesus, he said, "Lord, I will use this ministry to help the bereaved. I can sing for the funerals, and I can conduct the services. That will be confirming my friendship to you."

He felt the still, quiet voice of Jesus answer, "That is close to your commitment, though not quite to what I have called you. But go ahead. It will help you prepare for what I have called you to do."

A missionary in the hometown Baptist church also encouraged the young man. She said, "You will be good in this profession, and I will help you through mortuary school. Then you will be able to establish your own business."

And so the journey of life for this young man took another turn. He would spend several years in this ministry and profession. Life seemed to be going rather smoothly until the catalyst of war erupted. This time the call became personal, and the young man was obligated to change direction and serve in the United States Army.

Chapter

Seven

FACED WITH THE DILEMMA OF WAR ON THE battleground of life, the young man prayed, "Lord, I have been called to minister to the needs of our country. That is a task in which I can be a friend to you." Again, Jesus answered, "This is not your ministry, but it is closely related to your calling."

So the young man sold his mortuary business and responded to the call of his country. His earlier training as a mortician led to an assignment in the Army Medical Corps. There he was appointed to be a medic. He was stationed in Indiana where he received further training from the army as an anesthetist. This included training in surgical and medical procedures that would be used in overseas hospital duties.

CHAPTER

EIGHT

THE SOJOURN IN INDIANA WAS A HAPPY ONE, despite the anxieties of war. The young man sought out a Baptist fellowship and continued to attend church. On a certain Sunday, a young woman noted his uniform and invited him out to eat with some friends. It was wartime. Feelings and relationships were built quickly, for who could know what lay around the next corner? Often actions were impetuous. And so this friendship ripened quickly into courtship. They were married, and a daughter was born to this union.

Neither the man nor the woman had considered his or her goals or where their journey might lead. At this point, the young man surely thought that his dreams were lost amid the crises of war, marriage, and starting a family. The circumstances of his life had dictated changes in direction that no one could possibly have predicted.

Perhaps he would never become a minister of the gospel as he had dreamed, but he would always remain a friend to Jesus. But God, who knows all things and works all things together for good to those who love him and are called according to his purpose, knew that in the heart of the woman was also a dream—that she would someday marry a preacher and minister by his side (cf. Rom. 8:28).

Surely the Lord must have smiled as he beheld their little child. Even as she bound the couple together, so would she also be the Lord's instrument to bring to pass in his own time the appointed ministries.

CHAPTER

NINE

THE BABY WAS SCARCELY BORN BEFORE THE young medic was shipped to an overseas hospital in the European campaign. As the army hospital set up to receive the wounded, the soldier ever looked for opportunities to show his friendship. As he worked in Germany, he eagerly learned the language of the people. He was quick to take advantage of educational opportunities. When the hospital moved to England, he enrolled to study at the prestigious Oxford University.

The saw, an unlikely tool for either a soldier or a medic, was initially left behind. However, as the soldier began to see needs, he requested that he be allowed to send for it. The reply came that the saw could not be sent because it was too long to meet wartime postal regulations. Undaunted, Congress was entreated to allow this tool passage. A special Act of Congress finally delivered the saw to its owner.

From that time on, the saw became a part of the man. It was used to build hastily thrown together field hospitals. It was played to bring peace aboard the ship on storm-tossed seas. It was played in audience before Parliament in England. And always, it testified to the fact that this soldier was a friend to Jesus.

What's that in your hand?

Oh, nothing, my Lord,
Just a stick when I'm tired or alone
Or to keep the sheep safe from harm;
Nothing special; just a stick that I own.

The Lord must have chuckled a bit to himself
For only the Lord could see
What that stick that Moses held in his hand
Could do and what it could be.

For the things God can use seem foolish to men
As He comes all down through the years;
And asks that same question again and again
With answer to so many fears.

A saw, a whistle, an old brown jug,
Bring joy from the Father's heart;
Such little things, just common and old,
Yet transformed when he has a part!

CHAPTER

TEN

BY 1945, THE WAR HAD TAKEN ITS TOLL. MANY men did not come home. Those who did would never be the same. This gentle Georgia boy was so very weary from the violence of war and sickness and death of those to whom he had ministered so faithfully.

Upon returning to the homeland, the man received his honorable discharge from the military. But he would never be able to just take up life where he left it. Two long years of utter devastation had robbed him of his youth.

That time he'd lose, he thought in vain
Would never for him be;
That sadness, loss, or pain would come
He closed his eyes to see.

Yet come they did, and then he hid,
The conflict much too great
His dreams came tumbling down like rain
Too much was this, his fate.

Yet from the ashes of defeat
His dreams would slowly rise
Would cast their rays to season life
Even through his compromise.

He now needed only to get far away, to begin his life all over again. Education had proved comfortable for this young man, and the lure of faraway places called to him. He took his wife and daughter and journeyed westward as he willingly accepted the army's offer to go back to school and entered into yet another vocation: business administration.

Although this was not preaching, he rationalized that he could still be a friend to Jesus by offering families a financial plan for their future. Again, Jesus responded, "This is not what I have called you to do, but go ahead. It will give you good preparation for my calling."

CHAPTER

ELEVEN

THE MAN SETTLED HIS WIFE AND DAUGHTER IN Reno, Nevada, where he would attend the University of Nevada and study business administration. After graduation from the university, he accepted a job in a local bank.

Several years went by in this occupation. The family was blessed with a second child, a son. It would seem by outward appearance that earlier dreams and commitments were all but forgotten. But the "Spirit of the Friend" was already quickening to prepare the next step.

The ugly head of materialism was beginning to surface. The man saw those who misused and abused their resources. He realized that these persons were not seeking spiritual advice. They were scoffers and derelicts. Jesus could not be served in such an environment.

Nor was God's hand confined to the man. A little child was awakening to the redemption story: a book with only four pages—the first page, black as night, a picture of her sin; the second, red like crimson, the blood that precious Jesus shed for her wrongdoing; the third, her life made white as snow as she began to trust and obey; and finally the fourth, a picture of heaven with streets of pure gold.

"Mother," the disturbed child in puzzlement inquired, "Why did a good man like Jesus have to die for my sin?"

Quietly, gently, by her bedside, the little child accepted the atonement of her Lord, and one more small candle was lit for all eternity.

"Daddy, please go to Sunday School with us," she begged.

It was difficult to shake the habit of sleeping late on Sunday morning. Perhaps the quiet trust of his daughter rekindled his own spiritual hunger as he could clearly see Jesus through her childlike faith. Or perhaps the constancy of a loving wife reawakened him to his deep friendship with a gracious Savior. Surely he was touched by the love of God's people and the kindly pastor who nurtured and watered the seeds of ministry planted so long ago.

Once again, God gently called him out of complacency to the gospel ministry. Like Abraham and Moses so long ago, the journey of preparation had taken unlikely turns. It had taken forty years to prepare, but the Georgia boy was again headed toward his commitment to ministry.

CHAPTER

TWELVE

ONCE THE DECISION HAD BEEN MADE, NOTHING would stand in the way. Everything that could be eliminated was sold. The man, with his wife, daughter, and son, began the trek back and forth across the country, ever seeking God's guidance in their appointed calling. The journey was not easy as they traveled across the desert and over the great divide until they reached Texas. There they found a place near the great dome of Seminary Hill in Fort Worth.

A lifelong appreciation for music led to preparation for music ministry. While the man studied to develop his voice, he served a small country church in the John T. White Community.

Nevertheless, during his three years in seminary, they struggled to survive. Often, they did not know how bills would be paid. But over and over, they found God able and faithful to finish the work that he had ordained them to do. The rent would be due, and a check for just that amount would be in the mail with a note that the donor had felt God had led him to send it. The cupboards would be bare, and a church would decide the family needed groceries, a practice fondly called "pounding the preacher." So many encouragements came as the man began his journey back into The Plan.

The seminary years were a family experience. Perhaps no one grew any more during that time than the little girl who had embraced her daddy's Jesus and who walked in her daddy's footsteps.

Here prayer began to grow in the heart of the child. While the man's daughter enjoyed God's provisions for the family, she also learned to trust him to meet her personal needs. For example, it was a small matter for her God to restore a canine comrade who had wandered away. She learned she could trust her God for everything.

Her daddy quickly recognized his child's love for the old songs of faith and began to use the seminary practice rooms to teach her to play the piano. They often talked of their wonderful Jesus, and they memorized Scriptures together. As they stood together in the balcony of the great seminary rotunda and surveyed the mosaic map of the world on the floor below, together they sensed the spiritual hunger of a lost and dying world.

Ever after, when the child sang, "I'll Go Where You Want Me To Go, Dear Lord," she would envision that great map of faraway lands where there were those who needed to know Jesus. She knew, through the innocent vision of a child, that she could never be anything other than a missionary for Jesus. The dream of ministry was kindled again.

Training for the music ministry was nearly complete. In the early morning hours before the man was to perform his senior recital, another son was added to the family. The oratorio of praise he had selected held very special meaning as he left his wife and newborn son to complete the performance that would bring this chapter to a close.

CHAPTER

THIRTEEN

FORMAL TRAINING WAS COMPLETED, AND THE family was ready to leave Southwestern Baptist Theological Seminary and Fort Worth, Texas. Their journey led them to cross again the mountains westward, this time into northern California. As they traveled, the family sang together to pass the miles. The chorus, "Maranatha" (The Lord Comes), became a theme song. Over and over again, their voices raised in praise, thanksgiving, and victory. They sang in rounds and in parts. "For health and strength and daily bread, we give our thanks, Oh, Lord, our God." "Do Lord, oh, do Lord, oh do remember me." "I've got a mansion just over the hilltop." "Give me oil in my lamp, keep me burning . . . keep me burning 'til the break of day." And on and on they went. Each new chorus added to their repertoire.

The man's unique ability with the musical saw led into camp ministry. Those were wonderful days of fellowship when many young people were led to know Jesus as their personal Savior and Lord.

However, the environment for growing asparagus crops in California proved to be unhealthy, so the family again turned eastward until they finally arrived in Missouri to stay a short time with the wife's parents who had recently purchased a farm near LaMonte.

They found the old farm was in need of much repair. The Georgia man quickly began to use his carpentry skills. During this interlude, they were led to attend the First Baptist Church of Sweet Springs where God had placed an elderly preacher who immediately saw potential and intuitively guided the younger man to seek out the church ministry that God had prepared for him. Through this encouragement, dreams became reality. The man accepted a call to preach from Memorial Baptist Church near Sedalia, Missouri, in Harmony Baptist Association.

He was, at last, ordained to the gospel ministry at the First Baptist Church of Sweet Springs, Missouri. As he stood, the hand of his Friend brushed his shoulder, and he heard in himself, "This is my beloved child in whom I am well pleased." With this confirmation, he launched into the sweetest years of his lifetime.

CHAPTER

FOURTEEN

AS SO OFTEN HAPPENS, AFTER A TIME OF mountaintop experiences, the path can lead down into some valleys. The first parsonage in Postal, Missouri, was just such an encounter. For the pastor's wife, a refined city girl for much of her life, the challenge entailed a run-down house at the remote end of "rattlesnake lane," far too small for three children, with no running water, a kerosene cooking stove, live chickens to be killed and dressed to feed the family, only a one-room schoolhouse for her school-age son and daughter, a husband so enthralled with his work that he was seldom home, and another baby on the way! Surely she must have wondered, at times, if she or her husband had really heard God's call right.

But never did she convey any doubt or negative thought to her children. She accepted her role as pastor's wife with cheerfulness and dignity. She quietly supported her husband. She lifted her spirits and hardened into a true pioneer. She promoted missionary projects and encouraged her daughter to look to her for the inspiration of a godly woman.

My Mother taught her children well
To love the Lord and conquer self;
To serve His church and give the most;
Nor cry when others thoughtless boast.

First on the line when others hurt;
First to offer to clean up the dirt.
My mother taught her children well;
It's easy to see: their lives do tell.

This daughter, with her parents' inspiration and the help of the Lord, continued to grow in service. She learned to type and helped her dad put out a church bulletin. The family continued to sing and serve together. Regardless of the circumstances, this child knew herself to be "A Child of the King." "A tent or a cottage; why should I care? He's building a mansion for me over there." She continued to memorize Scripture. The story of Queen Esther and the words of Proverbs 31 became very special as she tried hard to become all God wanted her to be.

However, life in Missouri was not all sunshine. The frequent moves had traumatic effects on the family. Many valued possessions had been left behind. As the family took on the roles expected, much of the closeness of seminary days was lost. Life was lived under scrutiny. Close friendships were nonexistent. In spite of outward appearances, seeds of bitterness began to swell and fester, particularly in the children. As the girl entered her teen years, more and more sorrows were silently shared with the Lord.

Notwithstanding, God blessed the work as the ministry to Memorial Baptist Church came to be marked by several accomplishments. The new pastor began to initiate house-to-house visitation, and the church experienced outstanding growth as a result.

As the church grew in numbers, God met many needs. The pastor was moved into a new parsonage in a better school district. The church entered into a building program to raise the church and put a basement under it. As the members of the small struggling church learned to pray, the prayer life of the church became strong.

While at Memorial, a second daughter was born, bringing the family total to six persons. The work at Memorial had been well established. The Lord revealed his plan to go to another body of believers who would need the special touch of this servant. No one was more happy than the older daughter who saw in the move an opportunity to grow, to begin life anew, and to leave behind difficult social and emotional struggles.

CHAPTER

FIFTEEN

THE PREACHER HAD BEEN CALLED TO MINISTER to a small-town church in Lincoln, Missouri. The First Baptist Church of Lincoln was filled with new experiences unlike those of his rural ministry.

In Lincoln, his older daughter was able to take organ lessons to complement her growing proficiency at the keyboard. She also began to develop a social life. She was able to participate in Bible Drills and in the State Speakers' Tournament. As a high school junior, she excelled in her studies and was selected to participate in Missouri Girls' State. Many positive experiences tapped the potential in the young girl.

Yet, deep-seated emotional hurts also took their toll. Members of the congregation criticized the pastor and his family. Some even questioned their choice to own a dog. The preacher would allow no stumbling block to hinder his ministry. It was not important that the teenage girl had come to dote on the affectionate spaniel as her own special friend and confidante in a world where long-term friendships had been denied. No consideration was given to the stabilizing role the animal had played in her life. Many sacrifices were made but none so devastating as the loss of the dog.

In her frustration, she became painfully aware of friction and hypocrisy in the church family. Her perspectives turned inward as her ideology of Christian ministry began to deteriorate. She spent more and more time alone; her pride in achievement was only a cover for the heartaches that lay within.

As divisions and strife began to tear at the very heart of the preacher, he turned ever more intimately to his friend Jesus. Through many struggles, his prayer life and his leadership of other Christians in prayer continued to grow. As people learned to pray, they also learned to give themselves to others.

At Lincoln, the preacher had the privilege of starting a new work through a lake-area mission. Unlike many churches, this church had learned the secret of serving. As they ministered to the lake area, they sent the best that the church could offer. The church pianist, the church music director, the chairman of deacons, and others who formed the leadership of the home church went to form a nucleus at the mission. The Edmundson Mission thrived and grew as it reached out to many on the Lake of the Ozarks. It soon became a thriving community church.

The larger community also offered opportunity to be involved in hospital visitation, and his prior medical training gave this preacher a unique insight into ways to minister to families in times of sickness. The time to move came all too quickly as God again shifted direction through yet another church fellowship in another community.

CHAPTER

SIXTEEN

THE FIRST BAPTIST CHURCH AT HOLDEN, Missouri, was of similar size. But the community had the flavor of the larger metropolitan areas near Kansas City.

The first-born graduated from Holden High School. With great pride, the man watched this young woman enroll in college. Southwest Baptist College in Bolivar, Missouri, had been chosen because of its spiritual atmosphere. Unaware of the doubts and resentment that continued to torment his daughter, the preacher saw only a drive and determination to complete her commitment to the Lord. "Yes," he thought, "she will make a fine missionary." He avidly followed her progress as she led prayer and Bible groups and served the college as dorm counselor.

Then the day came when she announced she had a boyfriend. The preacher looked the boy over and was appalled. He could not believe she would turn aside her dream. This was no preacher student. He had none of the preconceived attributes that such a father would expect. He immediately discouraged this relationship in every way that he could. He could only hope that time would bring an end to the relationship he viewed as disastrous.

During this time of turbulence, another son was born to the preacher. He smiled as he dreamed of all the experiences he could now share with another precious member in his family.

Meanwhile, to the naive, sheltered preacher's daughter, the young man she had come to know represented all she wanted in a husband. He was gentle and understanding. He accepted all her social deficiencies and turbulent moods. He saw her as she was and gave his love unconditionally. His German roots of hard work, loyalty to God, family, and country, and his quiet ways beckoned to her. With this young man, she felt safe and complete.

Father and daughter, each so close to God's call, sought every opportunity to reconcile. They prayed constantly for each other and for God's intervention.

The young woman transferred to Ouachita Baptist University in Arkadelphia, Arkansas. There, she and her intended husband searched carefully for God's guidance. Very carefully, they examined each area of their lives and took steps toward the day that they could make that ultimate commitment to each other through the bond of marriage. Through the months of courtship, they realized how important it would be to their future to be reconciled with both sets of their parents. The girl's strong religious background made it imperative that they unite in their faith as well as in their lifestyles.

As the families grew better acquainted, God's peace came to rest once more. By now, the preacher saw promise in this young man. How true, he observed, that man looks on outward appearance, but only God can see the heart (cf. 1 Sam. 16:7). The time came when the preacher proudly baptized his future son-in-law, and it was his pleasure to unite the couple in a Christmas wedding.

The ministry in Holden continued to grow through prayer and visitation. It was a new adventure to drive to Iowa to transport a baptistry from the factory and then to install it.

Another highlight in the ministry was when the church voted to send their pastor to participate in the Missouri-Australia Crusade. The entire church family participated weeks ahead by sending letters to prospects in Australia. For six weeks, the pastor introduced his friend Jesus and played his musical saw across the continent down under. As a result, hundreds came to make decisions for Christ.

Life was fulfilling in so many ways, but it was time to move once again.

CHAPTER

SEVENTEEN

THE NEW ASSIGNMENT TO THE FIRST BAPTIST Church of Lilbourn, Missouri, was an unusual assignment for a pastor because its focus was on persons outside the church family. There, this preacher found a very special group of men.

These men had spent their lifetimes in being apart from anything religious. Many were already suffering the ill effects from years of alcoholism. There were not many of God's chosen instruments who would be able to relate to these men. To this preacher, the cotton fields they farmed brought memories of boyhood days in the fields of Georgia. Their errant lifestyles were not unlike those he had encountered in Reno, Nevada, before the days of ministry, or those of Fort Worth, Texas, as he helped a young church to grow. The frequent fishing trips they enjoyed together reminded him of his commitment to Jesus who called to disciples of long ago, "Follow me, and I will make you fishers of men" (Matt. 4:19). God had chosen a special servant who had been training for nearly fifty years.

> To all who need a Savior,
> My Friend I recommend,
> Because He bro't salvation,
> Is why I am His friend.

By this time, the daughter had been married for over a year. Both she and her husband had graduated from college. Her husband's time of military deferment was at an end. He, therefore, situated his young bride with a widowed aunt near St. Louis, Missouri, and entered officer's training in Fort Knox, Kentucky.

During this year of separation, the girl tried her hand at teaching third grade in a small consolidated school. She found the task to be enjoyable and stimulating. She also enjoyed frequent trips to visit her parents and family. Although she attended services regularly with the aunt, her personal faith began to slowly fade away.

Upon graduation from officer's training, the young lieutenant received orders to go to Germany. Since the time of separation had gone well and bills from college were still being paid, the couple decided to continue the teaching position until the end of the school year when the wife would join her husband overseas.

However, years of spiritual neglect had taken their toll, and the young woman had unknowingly set herself up to fall. She had begun depending on antidepressants to combat loneliness and depression. An acquaintance took advantage of her weaknesses and made improper advances. By February she was taking more and more drugs. On the verge of a complete breakdown, she called her parents. They came immediately. Necessary arrangements were made, and the young woman was able to join her husband three months earlier than planned, feeling very much a failure.

Ever true to his Friend, the preacher continued to show the community by his actions and his words how precious Jesus was to him. He pled with those who would listen to come meet his Savior. Many did turn away from former lives as they accepted the gift of eternal life through Jesus Christ.

On the world scene, the Vietnam conflict was raging. Word of casualties began to come in—first a close friend, then a dear nephew. So many families were touched by grief. And the preacher continued to minister to their needs.

The preacher and his wife had barely heard the good news that their older daughter was expecting a child when the word came that a tiny casket was being flown for burial to St. Louis. With heavy hearts, they made the unwanted trip to pay final respects to the grandchild they would never know.

The failures of the past and the heartaches of the present became too heavy for the daughter to bear. She threw herself into the parties and revelry of an army wife to try to forget. Her God seemed so very far away.

Then came the unwelcome orders that her soldier-husband had been reassigned to Vietnam. The thirty-day leave he had been granted went by far too quickly. The preacher alone knew how to comfort this one who was being sent to battle.

For his daughter, it was again a time to start anew. She applied for a position with her old school. She rented her own apartment. This time she was able to resist any temptation that would take her off course. She devoted her efforts to her students, her church, and her family. Her failures were turned into victories as she looked back to the Lord for her strength. And yet the shadows of years past and the loss of her firstborn haunted her days.

During this time, Satan began to work within the church at Lilbourn to divide and conquer. The gift of the

Holy Spirit, given freely to all who believe to work unity in the church, was perverted by some to create division. Many unkind words were hurled. While a lost community looked on, the preacher was driven to seek early retirement.

> Little seeds dropped one by one,
> Slowly through the years they come;
> Eating away at happiness,
> Leaving all to watch and guess
> What could have happened to all the dreams?
> What went wrong with dreams and schemes?

But God had not abandoned his servant, the preacher, his church, or the preacher's daughter.

CHAPTER

EIGHTEEN

THE OLDEST DAUGHTER AND HER HUSBAND, only briefly back from Vietnam, sadly came to move a wounded soldier of the Lord to a place of comfort. While in Vietnam, the young soldier had experienced the touch of the living God. The Lord's presence became very real to him while he lay sheltered in a bunker. During those hallowed moments, the man, following the steps of his father-in-law so long before, made the personal commitment that he would always be a friend to Jesus.

Subsequently, the daughter and her husband accepted what would be only a year's sojourn in the small community of Sullivan, Missouri. There God had placed one of his special servants, a pastor who daily walked with his Lord. His quiet, gentle leadership proved to be a healing balm to this couple, once again setting them on the path to ministry.

Though the ministry in Lilbourn had not been completed, the Lord led the preacher to settle with his remaining family in the small southwestern Missouri community of Seymour. This would be the final move. Yet it was by no means the end of the man's preaching ministry. It was rather the start of a ministry to small rural churches around the town of Seymour that were not so unlike those churches from the early years in Georgia.

He served first at Antioch. Then at the Pleasant Ridge Church, he used his expertise in plumbing to install a water system and indoor bathrooms.

At the First Baptist Church of Seymour, he served as a layperson and chairman of the missions committee. Through his lifelong interest in missions, he encouraged others to become interested in mission giving.

Always open to opportunities, he also began to transport mentally handicapped children to a state school in Marshfield, Missouri. While the children were learning, the man spent time in ministry to senior adults at the Marshfield Senior Center. During this time, he discovered that many of those around the center were lonely with little to challenge them or bring cheer. So the man initiated a "kitchen" band to encourage them.

He was soon asked to extend his musical talents as director for the Marshfield Older Americans' Band. This group exuded life and vitality through their lively renditions of the old folk songs. Every instrument was welcome from bird whistles to violin, from piano to an old brown jug, from guitar to the old washboard. The saw continued to be used as a part of this ministry.

During this period, the preacher saw his older daughter and son-in-law follow the seminary trail into camp ministry. Their joy was made full with the miracle birth of a long-awaited son.

The preacher was no less proud of his second child. This son had chosen the career of master craftsman to rebuild grand pianos for the enjoyment of others. His middle son had surrendered to the gospel ministry. What joy it brought to see his labors continued through this son.

He radiated in the sunshine of his younger daughter's smile. He reveled in the exuberance of his youngest son. The house did not lack for joy and warmth.

The old man grew to treasure each special birthday or holiday as patriarch of such a wonderful family. His grandchildren lit up his life. Life in semiretirement could not be better. A new chapter was surely beginning.

CHAPTER

NINETEEN

THE CEDAR GAP CHURCH, ONLY FIVE MILES from Seymour, had earlier experienced a burnout. The congregation decided to rebuild on a plot of land that bordered the new divided highway. They intended their church to be a lighthouse for those who would pass by. Travelers were welcomed.

When the Cedar Gap Church asked the preacher to become their interim pastor, he readily accepted another opportunity to preach the gospel, but it was soon evident that the church needed a man who could share the sense of mission. So what had begun as temporary became permanent. The church called this man, his wife by his side, to be their pastor.

So many years of married bliss
Sealed by God and a tender kiss.
Years may come and years may go
Lives entwined just grow and grow.

Seems only a day since the first was born
A promise of love in a world-war town.
Four more to come in measured time,
Each a lifetime down the line.

Now they all have gone their ways
And time moves on with a thousand rays.
So many memories, sweet and sad,
In life together have they had.

His eyes now tired and dimmed with time,
Still speak to her in tones sublime:
"Come sit by my side for a little while."
She feels his plea and turns with smile.

So hand in hand and thought to thought
They enter the twilight as they ought.
A life well spent in service and love
Continues to labor for God above.

The major emphases at Cedar Gap were to build a prayer force in the congregation and to promote a deep Christian love for one another. Transients soon found this fellowship to be quick to respond to need, in prayer and action. A prayer chain linked members together in a bond of communion.

The church grew and began to improve its facilities. The basement was remodeled into classrooms and a fellowship hall. The bathrooms were updated. A baptistry was installed. New classrooms and a vestibule were added to the main floor.

In the midst of all this, a single event brought into clear focus all the training and experiences of life. It happened through a unique and unlikely friendship with another older couple. The couple owned a few run-down buildings that had at one time served as a dry-goods store. They had no family. They seemed all alone, eccentric in many of their ways, and had little to offer. The preacher found that the man was in failing health though he still drove the old car they owned and took care of all the meager finances for his wife.

By this time, all the children had gone from the preacher's home, so the two couples grew to enjoy each other's company. As their friendship grew, the sickly gentleman began to be concerned about what would happen to his wife when he passed on. It was only natural that he would ask his preacher friend to look out for her.

So the time came that the sick man passed away, but what a surprise was in store! Administration of so little unfolded day by day into a massive fortune. The wife had had no idea of her husband's dealings through the years. All the business skills, knowledge of stocks and bonds, the mortuary, farming, all were drawn upon to put the sizable estate into usable order.

And God smiled as his servant realized another lesson—that nothing in God's economy is ever wasted (cf. Matt. 15:37).

CHAPTER

TWENTY

THE INTERVENING YEARS HAD NOT GONE nearly so well, however, for the daughter. She and her husband had been so very happy in service at the state Baptist encampment. A year had quickly turned to four. The next logical step seemed to be that of directing new mission encampments in Peru. How excited the couple was as they anticipated appointment. When the Foreign Mission Board turned down their application, the young woman was hurt and embittered. All the resentments of childhood were exposed as fresh wounds. In their frustrations, they began to take sides in dissension within the camp. Complaints and discord brought with it more discontent. The couple decided it was time to move.

After only a brief stay with the Missouri Baptist Children's Home in St. Louis, the couple accepted charge of a Baptist Emergency Shelter in Brownsville, Texas. Located only eleven blocks from the border, the environment was more Mexican than American. Numerous trials, theft of material possessions, loneliness, and hardships in this wilderness experience molded the couple into more usable vessels. The young woman especially developed a new grace and character. The couple was almost ready to accept God's ministry in any situation.

After a very hard year and ten months in this mission, the couple again packed and headed for home. Awaiting them in Van Buren, Missouri, was a regional encampment. God had brought them full circle to the ministry they had deserted.

A year or so had gone by when circumstances indicated that major surgery was needed to remove diseased ovaries and uterus. During the time of recuperation, the young woman became very depressed. Her husband seemed happy enough, but she still could not accept God's call to the remote, broken-down facility. The work was physically difficult and emotionally demanding. But most of all, this mission simply did not measure up to the expectations and dreams she had had through the years of missionary service. In this crisis of belief, God spoke to her, unmistakably calling her back unto himself. With tears in her eyes, she reaffirmed, "I'll be content wherever you place me, Lord. Forgive me and use me as you will." This experience, as God brought new perspectives, was a turning point in her ministry.

Life continued to present ups and downs. An adopted daughter filled the void created by loss of a child. Then came a dark period of trials. Within eight months, there was a serious car accident involving her parents, loss of a job, death of her brother, death of a beloved grandmother, her husband's heart attack and subsequent double bypass surgery, and elopement of her daughter. Each new circumstance drew the couple into a closer relationship as they drew strength from Jesus and accepted the ministry to which they had been appointed.

The preacher had, meanwhile, served as pastor of Cedar Gap for nine years; the time had come for final retirement. His health was now failing. His heart had been nearly broken as he lost his preacher son to cancer.

Still, life was not without compensation. He was able to make one last journey to his beloved Georgia to put life in perspective. He had seen his older daughter follow her commitment to serve in missions. His oldest son owned a successful business and had a beautiful family of his own. His younger daughter and her family were so adept at ministering to their daily needs. What a wonder that his youngest son would be able to take a mission trip to Romania.

This tired, old preacher continued to use his influence encouraging and supporting others. Even when health was gone, he continued financial support that the Lord's work could go on—and so it did.

CHAPTER

TWENTY-ONE

IN JUNE 1992, THE FAMILY WAS TOLD THAT THEIR husband-father was suffering from carcinoma cancer in the form of two small tumors close to his heart. Because of location, the tumors were inoperable.

As father and daughter sat side by side in the darkened living room, she reached for his hand and reassured him simply, "Daddy, you have showed us how to live; now it is time to show us how to die."

The weeks became months, and the body began to close down its earthly functions in preparation for that final chapter of life. He accepted his daughter's challenge and the finality of his diagnosis.

Shortly before his death, the preacher called his daughter to his side and commissioned her to write his story. As he had carefully fitted the pieces together, he saw clearly, as in a vision, his life spent with his friend Jesus.

There had been many vocations, but only one calling, throughout his life. The segments of his life separated clearly into twenty-one chapters. To this preacher's mind, the significance of the numerical factors was clear: the number three, the Godhead; and the number seven, the symbol of his completed life; when multiplied together, the product was peace.

And in that peace, he described the angels who came to take him to his eternal home. He caught glimpses of that heavenly place that he could only describe as beautiful. His example, as he made the heavenly transition, took away all fear of death for those around him.

The man's indomitable spirit continued to be strong even in the face of death itself. His Shepherd in life was all the more present as he made final preparations to cross over the great divide and meet his Savior and Friend face to face.

EPILOGUE

BY SEPTEMBER 1992, WE ALL KNEW THAT MY dad's death was imminent. We also knew that he had fought a good fight and was ready to finish the course of faith. When Dad called me to his side and told me of his plans for a book, I knew it was important to him to bring life to an appropriate close—to allow even his death to be an encouragement to others.

He read the first draft of the book he had envisioned. "It is good," he pronounced. "But you have omitted your story."

"But Daddy," I objected, "my life is not finished. How can I include it? This is your story."

"I will show you," he promised. And he did. As he looked back on his life, he could see so clearly the patterns that God had interwoven through the years.

And as I wrote, I discovered that the same God who had so carefully patterned and used my dad had also woven his careful pattern in me. And it is so with everyone who will yield his/her life to be molded by the Master's hand.

This preacher truly discovered the joy of being a friend to Jesus. His story is intended to encourage and challenge every person to seize any opportunity to be of service to Jesus—no matter how small or insignificant that service might seem at the time.

On November 7, 1992, my dad passed on into new life with his Friend Jesus. This book is the story of that great friendship as he related it to me both in word and in deed. In so many ways, he said to us all, "I'd like you to meet my friend, Jesus."

—Mary Ann Bruening